MIDLOTHIAN
PUBLIC LIBRARY

W9-BZV-690

Indy Cars

Kate Riggs

MIDLOTHIAN PUBLIC LIBRARY
14701 S. KENTON AVE.
MIDLOTHIAN, IL 60445

seedlings

CREATIVE EDUCATION • CREATIVE PAPERBACKS

Published by Creative Education and Creative Paperbacks
P.O. Box 227, Mankato, Minnesota 56002
Creative Education and Creative Paperbacks are
imprints of The Creative Company
www.thecreativecompany.us

Design by Ellen Huber
Production by Chelsey Luther
Printed in the United States of America

Photographs by Corbis (Robert Baker/AP, William
Manning), Dreamstime (Sergei Bachlakov, Dwebrown,
Raja Rc, Sideline), Getty Images (DAVID BOILY/AFP, Jon
Feingersh, Mark Thompson), iStockphoto (Hirkophoto,
Rutryin), Newscom (Jose Carlos Fajardo/MCT), Shutterstock
(Brian Patterson Photos, carroteater, Digitalstormcinema,
Iryna Rasko, STILLFX, YaiSirichai), SuperStock (Oleksiy
Maksymenko/All Canada Photos)

Copyright © 2015 Creative Education, Creative Paperbacks
International copyright reserved in all countries.
No part of this book may be reproduced in any form
without written permission from the publisher.

Library of Congress Cataloging-in-Publication Data
Riggs, Kate.
Indy cars / Kate Riggs.
p. cm. — (Seedlings)
Summary: A kindergarten-level introduction to Indy cars,
covering their speed, drivers, role in racing sports, and such
defining features as their wings.
Includes index.
ISBN 978-1-60818-520-7 (hardcover)
ISBN 978-1-62832-120-3 (pbk)
1. Indy cars—Juvenile literature. I. Title.

TL236.R493 2014
629.228—dc23   2014000181

CCSS: RI.K.1, 2, 3, 4, 5, 6, 7;
RI.1.1, 2, 3, 4, 5, 6, 7; RF.K.1, 3; RF.1.1

First Edition
9 8 7 6 5 4 3 2 1

TABLE OF CONTENTS

Time to race!

Indy cars
are fast cars.

They race on oval tracks. They race on roads.

Indy cars have four big wheels.

The wheels are not covered.

Indy cars have parts called wings. One wing is on the front. The other is on the back.

One person drives an Indy car. The driver sits in the cockpit.

Indy cars race
each other.
They try to
be faster than
the other cars.

An Indy
car speeds
around a
track. It stops
at the pit for
more gas.

Go, Indy car,

go!

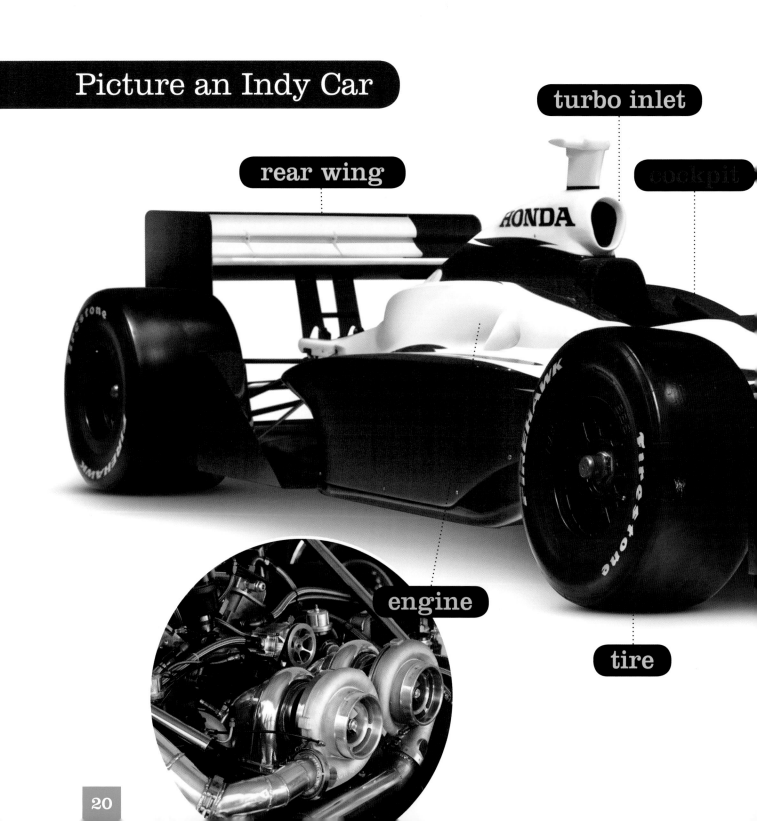

Picture an Indy Car

turbo inlet

rear wing

cockpit

engine

tire

x1000r/min

tachometer

FIREHAWK

front wing

Words to Know

cockpit: the place where a race-car driver sits

oval: shaped like an egg

pit: the part of a racetrack where cars go to get more gas or have something fixed

Read More

David, Jack. *Indy Cars.*
Minneapolis: Bellwether Media, 2008.

Mason, Paul. *Indy Cars.*
Mankato, Minn.: Amicus, 2011.

Websites

Hot Wheels Pit Race Off
http://www.hotwheels.com/en-us/games/pit-race.html
Pretend you are an Indy car driver, and race your own car!

Indy Car Coloring Pages
http://indykids.tripod.com/
Learn more about Indy car history, and print pages to color.

Note: Every effort has been made to ensure that the websites listed above are suitable for children, that they have educational value, and that they contain no inappropriate material. However, because of the nature of the Internet, it is impossible to guarantee that these sites will remain active indefinitely or that their contents will not be altered.

Index